Brown and Foster

The Strangers' Guide

And Complete Hand Book through the City of New York

Brown and Foster

The Strangers' Guide
And Complete Hand Book through the City of New York

ISBN/EAN: 9783337213152

Printed in Europe, USA, Canada, Australia, Japan

Cover: Foto ©Andreas Hilbeck / pixelio.de

More available books at **www.hansebooks.com**

INDEX.

Map of New York.
Hackney Coach Fare.
To Hotels.
    Banks, Insurance and Express Offices.
    Lawyers, Brokers and Commission Merchants.
    Wholesale Dealers.
    Builders, Masons and Manufacturers.
    Machine Shops and Ship Yards.
    Principal Streets for Retailers.
    National Banks.
    Places of Amusements, with directions how to
        get there.
    Places of Interest, with directions, &c.
Map of Central Park.
Central and other Parks, with directions, &c.
Public Buildings, with directions, &c.
Offices of Daily Press.
Libraries.
Table of Distances from Battery to Harlem.
Ferry Landings.
Location of Piers.
Post-Office and Stations.
Steam R. R. Depots.
New York Markets.
Principal Express Companies.
Telegraph Companies.

TO THE PUBLIC.

In compiling and arranging this book, it has been the object to make its contents as plain and therefore as useful to strangers as a work of this kind can be made. There are many who visit the city, who from lack of knowledge of places of interest, leave again, without having seen anything but "bricks and mortar," whereas with a book of this nature in their pockets, they would have been enabled to learn and observe many of the city *sights*, without troubling their friends or asking strangers. Accompanying this little work is a fine *Map of the City* and famous *Central Park*. Confident that its issue meets a want long felt, the undersigned, without further remark, offer their "STRANGERS' GUIDE" to those whom pleasure or business may have called to the city, earnestly hoping that it will fully answer the purpose for which it is intended.

THE PUBLISHERS.

AN ORDINANCE

Amending the Ordinances, entitled "Ordinances for the Government of Hackney Coaches in the City of NewYork," passed May 5, 1848.

The Mayor, Aldermen, and Commonalty of the City of New York, in Common Council convened, do ordain as follows :

The Title Third of said Ordinance, shall be amended so as to read as follows :

TITLE THIRD OF THE RATES AND PRICES OF FARES.

The prices or rates of fares to be taken or paid to the owners or drivers of hackney coaches or carriages, shall be as follows :

1st. For conveying a passenger any distance not exceeding one mile, *fifty cents;* for conveying two passengers the same distance, *seventy-five cents,* or *thirty-seven and a half cents each ;* and for every additional passenger, *thirty-seven and a half cents.*

2d. For conveying a passenger any distance exceeding a mile, and within two miles, *seventy-five cents;* and for every additional passenger, *thirty-seven and a half cents.*

7

3d. For conveying a passenger to the new Alms-house and returning, *one dollar;* and for every additional passenger and returning, *fifty cents.*

4th. For conveying one passenger to Fortieth-street, and remaining half an hour, and returning, *one dollar and a half;* and for every additional passenger, *fifty cents.*

5th. For conveying one passenger to Sixty-first-street, and remaining three quarters of an hour, and returning, *two dollars;* and for every additional passenger, *fifty cents.*

6th. For conveying one passenger to Eighty-sixth-street, and remaining one hour, and returning, *two dollars and a half;* and for every additional passenger, *seventy-five cents.*

7th. For conveying one or more passengers to Harlem, and returning, with the privilege of remaining three hours, *five dollars;* or to the High Bridge, *five dollars,* with the same privilege.

8th. For conveying one or more passengers to Kings Bridge, and returning, with the privilege of keeping the carriage all day, *five dollars.*

9th. For the use of a hackney coach or carriage by the day, with one, or more passengers, *five dollars.*

10th. For the use of a hackney coach or carriage by the hour, with one or more passengers, with the privilege of going from place to place, and stopping as often as may be required, *one dollar an hour.*

11th. In all cases where the hiring of a hackney coach or carriage is not at the time thereof specified to be by the day or hour, it shall be deemed to be by the mile.

12th. For children between two and fourteen years of age, half price is only to be charged ; and for children under two years of age, no charge is to be made.

13th. Whenever a hackney coach or carriage shall be detained, excepting as aforesaid, the owner or driver shall be allowed after the rate of *seventy-five cents an hour.*

Adopted by the Board of Aldermen, April 16, 1853.

Adopted by the Board of Assistants, April 18th, 1853.

Adopted by the Mayor, April 24, 1853.

D. T. VALENTINE, Clerk, C. C.

HOTELS.

One of the first and most important objects to a visitor on his arrival in city of New York is to learn where a safe and convenient place can be found to put up. Knowing this, we have been very careful in this little book to note down some of the best hotels in the city, with their location :

Anson House, cor. of Spring and Crosby ;
Astor House, Broadway, cor. of Vesey ;
Broadway, cor. of Broadway and W. 22nd ;
Brandreth House, 292 Canal St. cor. of Broadway ;
Bancroft House, 906 Broadway ;
Brevort House, 11, 5th Av. ;
Barcelona, 23 Great Jones St.;
Courtlandt Street, 28 Courtlandt St. ;
Clarendon, 60 Union Place ;
Earls, 241 Canal St., near North river ;
Everett House, cor. of E. 17th and 4th Av. ;

———◆———

Fith Av., 192 5th Av., cor. of W. 23th St. ;
Gramercy Park, Cor. E. 20th and Gramercy Park ;
Howard House, 176 Broadway ;
Irving House, 45 E. 12th St. ;
Lafarge House, 673 Broadway ;
Madison Av., 85 Madison Av. ;
Merchants, 41 Courtlandt St. ;
Metropolitan, 580 Broadway ;
Prescott House, 531 Broadway ;
Park House,
St. Denis, 2 W. 12th St. ;
St. Germain, in 22th, cor. of Broadway and 5th Av.
(see Map.) ;
St. Nicholas, 515 Broadway ;
St. James, 1135 Broadway ;
Steven's House, 5 Union Place ;
Spingler House, 27 Broadway ;
United States, 200 Water ;
Union Place, cor. of Broadway and E. 14th St. ;
Western Hotel, 9 Courtlandt St. ;

Waverly Hotel, 697 Broadway ;
Westchester, cor. of Broome and Bowery.

KEPT ON EUROPEAN PLAN (MEALS WHERE YOU
PLEASE).

Albermarle, 1101 Broadway ·
Continental, 442 Broadway ;
French's, cor. of Frankfort and Chatham ;
Girard House, 129 Chamber St. ;
Hone House, 682 Broadway, cor. of Gr. Jones St. ;
International Hotel, 367 Broadway ;
Leggetts, Chatham, near Chamber St. ;
Lovejoys, 34 Park Row ;
Maillard House, 619 and 621 Broadway ;
Revere House, 606 Broadway ;
Sweeney's, 68 Chatham ;
Tamany, 166 Nassau.

After having secured Hotel accommodations, if your visit be for business purposes, it is a matter of time and importance to know that most of the

BANKS, INSURANCE & EXPRESS OFFICES

are to be found in the lower part of the city between Chambers Street and Battery, principally in lower part of Broadway and vicinity of Cedar, Pine, and Wall Streets.

LAWYERS OFFICES

are to be found in Nassau, Beekman, and William Streets, Broadway, just below Courtlandt St. and in the streets around the City Hall Park.

COMMISSION MERCHANTS,

in the vicinity of Liberty, Cedar, Pine, Wall, Broadway, and South William Streets and Exchange Place. These streets, together with all others constituting the lower portion of the city, are entirely devoted to business and can be reached by nearly every stage and car in the city.

WHOLESALE DEALERS

principally occupy the streets west of Broadway, below Canal St. and can be found scattered throughout the whole lower portion of the city.

BUILDERS, MASONS, AND MANUFACTURERS

can be found throughout the central portion of the city, from Broome to 40th Sts.

MACHINE SHOPS AND SHIP YARDS

are principally located along the river front above 4th St., North River and Houston St. East River.

FOR SHOPPING

the principal retail streets are Broadway, Canal, Hudson Sts. and 8th Av. on the West side.

On the *East*, Chatham, Bowery, and Grand Sts., and 3rd and 4th Avenues. In these streets can be found fabrics of every kind, from every portion of the world.

NATIONAL BANKS.

First, 131 Broadway ;   Fifth, 338 Third Av.
Central, 73 Duane ;   Sixth, W. 35th, cor. Bdw.;
Second, 5th Av. cor. W.   Eighth, 650 Broadway ;
   23d ;   Ninth, 363 Broadway ;
Fourth, 27 Pine ;   Tenth, 243 Broadway.

PLACES OF AMUSEMENT.

The following places offer a choice of recreation :

WALLACK'S THEATRE,

cor. of Broadway & 13th St.,

can be reached by the Broadway and 5th Av. line, Broadway and 42d St. line, Broadway and Wall St. line, Broadway, 23d St. and 9th Av. lines of Stages. All pass the entrance ; the 3d Av. cars (red), 4th Av. cars (yellow), the 42d St. E. Houston and Grand St. cars (green) pass within one block.

WINTER-GARDEN THEATRE,

(between Bleecker and Amity), 667 *Broadway,*

reached the same as Wallack's ; Broadway, Bleecker 23d St. and 8th Av. line, and 2d St. and Broadway cars pass cor. of Bleecker & Broadway, half a block of entrance.

OLYMPIC THEATRE,

624 Broadway, between Bleecker and Houston, can be reached by all Broadway stages.

NIBLO'S GARDEN THEATRE,

576 Broadway (cor. of Prince), can be reached by all Broadway stages.

BROADWAY THEATRE,

485 Broadway (near Broome), can be reached by all Broadway stages and Broadway University Place and 7th Av. cars (Broome St. branch).

OLD BOWERY THEATRE,

48 Bowery, between Canal and Bayard Sts.,

NEW YORK STADT THEATRE,

37 Bowery, between Canal and Hester Sts.,

and

THE NEW BOWERY THEATRE,

82 Bowery,

can be reached by 3d Av. cars, and the Bowery & Houston St., and Bowery, Av. C. and South Ferry lines of stages ; Grand St. Ferry, Broadway and Canal St. cars pass within half a block of each of their doors.

BARNUM'S AMERICAN MUSEUM,

Junction of Broadway and Ann St.,

can be reached by nearly every car and stage in the city.

BRYANT'S MINSTRELS,

472 Broadway, between Grand & Broome Sts.,

can be reached by Broadway stages, Grand & Canal St. stages, will stop on cor. of Grand St. & Broadway, a few doors from entrance, University Place, Broadway & 7th Av. cars (Broome St. branch), stopping on cor. of Broadway & Broome, half a block from the entrance.

WOOD'S MINSTRELS,

514 Broadway, between Broome & Spring,

can be reached by nearly all the Broadway stages, and within half a block by University Place, Broadway & 7th Av. cars (Broome Str. branch).

MUSEUM OF ANATOMY,

(open day and evening) 618 Broadway, between Houston & Bleecker Sts.,

can be reached same as Olympic.

ANATOMICAL MUSEUM,

(open day and evening) 51 *Chatham St.,*

THE ACADEMY OF MUSIC or ITALIAN OPERA HOUSE.

This magnificent building is situated on the corner of 14th St. & Irving Place,

can be reached by the same routes as Wallack's. During the operatic season the highest order of foreign talent is employed, and the seasons are generally prosperous.

And numbers of other places present innumerable attractions to the stranger. Among the prominent places of interest calculated to repay the visitors is first and greatest the now far famed

CENTRAL PARK.

The beauties of this charming resort need only to be seen to be appreciated. Under the direction of the energetic Commissioners all that a combination of wealth, labor, and skill can produce, may be enjoyed by a stroll through its pleasant walks and rambles, a sail upon its picturesque lakes or a view of its beautiful fountains. Extending in length from 59th to 110th Streets, in width from 5th to 8th Av., covering 850 acres. It is with the exception of the French Park, *Bois de Boulogne*, the largest and most splendid park in the world. The Croton reservoir, within its limits, occupies 106 acres and is 38 feet deep. The 6th, 7th, and 8th Av. and

Central Park cars take you to its gates, while the
3d Av. cars on the East side carry you to 72d St.
& 3d Av., two short blocks from its 5th Av. gate.
Among the many other Squares and Parks that will
amply repay the visit of the stranger is

MADISON SQUARE,

a large public park, located between 5th & Madison
Avenues & 23d to 26th Streets. Can be reached by
University Place, Broadway and 7th Av. cars, 42d
St. E. Houston & Grand St. cars. The Broadway
& 5th Av., Broadway and 42d St. stages all pass it.
Near this park, on the 5th Av. side, is located the

WORTH MONUMENT.

Next down town is

UNION PARK,

located on Broadway between 14th and 17th Sts.,
can be reached the same way as Madison Square,

P. MURPHY,

TAILOR AND DRAPER,

87 BLEECKER STREET,

NEAR BROADWAY,   NEW YORK.

the 4th Av. cars also pass it. Near the lower end, at the junction of 3d Av. & 14th St. is the fine equestrian statue of Washington.

WASHINGTON SQUARE,

located between Waverley Place and 4th, and Wooster & Mc Dougal Sts. (west side of the city), can be reached by University Place, Broadway & 7th Av. cars and by Amity St., 7th Av., and Fulton Ferry stages.

TOMPKINS SQUARE.

between 7th & 11th Sts. and Av. A. to B. (East side of the city), can be reached by Broadway, 8th St. and South Ferry line of stages. The 42d St. E. Houston & Grand St. line of cars pass it.

PROMINENT BUILDINGS.

CROTON RESERVOIR,

between 6th & Madison Av. and 40th & 42d Sts. can be reached by Broadway .& 42d St. (Madison Av.) stages and 6th Av. cars. University Place 7th Av. & Broadway cars, passing one block from it. Farther down town is the well known

COOPER INSTITUTE BUILDING,

on 8th St., between the 3d & 4th Av., can be reached by the 3d & 4th Av. cars; the Broadway & 5th Av., Broadway & 42d St., and Broadway & 4th Av. line of stages will set you down within a block of the doors.

POLICE HEADQUARTERS,

Mulberry St., between Bleecker & Houston Sts. The Broadway stages and 3d & 4th Av. cars run within a block or two of it.

THE TOMBS (City Prison),

a massive marble building, Egyptian architecture, located in Centre St., between Leonard & Franklin Sts. The 4th Av. & Fulton Ferry, Bleecker & 14th St. cars pass it; the Broadway stages run within three blocks of it.

CITY HOSPITAL,

Broadway, opposite Pearl St. Broadway stages pass it. Two blocks farther down is the

CITY HALL and PARK.

The City Hall contains Mayor's Office, the session rooms of Boards of Aldermen and Councilmen, County Clerks, City Library, Naturalization Office, and Governor's-room, generally used on public occasions, for receptions, &c. Hall of Records, containing City Comptroller's and Register's offices; the Rotunda, containing offices of Croton Aqueduct Department; the Court House (brown stone building), are all located in City Hall Park, and can be reached by all the cars and stages in the city, the following excepted : the Grand & Canal St. and Manhattanville & High Bridge stages ; the 42d & Grand St. ; the 2d Av. ; the Grand St. Ferry, Broadway & Canal St. ; the Central Park North & East river cars. All other *car* or *stage routes pass* or *terminate* in the *vicinity* of the *City Hall.*

Near the City Hall Park, and just below it, on the right hand side of Broadway, is the venerable *St. Paul's Church.* Farther down, about a quarter of a mile, on the same side of Broadway, directly opposite Wall St., is located

TRINITY CHURCH,

built upon the site of the old church in 1846, with its grand old church yard, and spire, reaching 284 feet high, from the top of which, by asking the attendant, you can obtain an interesting and extended view of the whole of the city, bay and surrounding country. Down Wall St., in the direction of East river, one block from Trinity, is the old

CUSTOM HOUSE BUILDING,

now used as the Sub-Treasury Department; about two blocks farther down Wall St., in the direction of the river, is the old

MERCHANT'S EXCHANGE,

now used as the Custom House. Two blocks in the rear, on the corner of William St. & Exchange Place, is the famous

GOLD ROOM

of New York, that regulates or irregulates during business hours the gold market of the country. Still farther down on the extreme lower end of the city, on the outer edge of the Battery, facing the bay, is located

CASTLE GARDEN,

originally built as a fort, then used as a place of recreation, but now doing duty as a receptacle for newly arrived emigrants. All the stages and cars marked South Ferry stop near this old edifice. From this point a ride in one of the Broadway stages up town will enable the visitor to note the lights and shades of a living panorama, that cannot be equaled for variety and attraction in any other portion of the world. Those who desire to see wonderful master pieces of mechanism, the printing presses of our daily newspapers, will be well satisfied by a visit to the *New York Herald* office, corner of Fulton & Nassau St.; the *New York Sun*, on the opposite corner; the *Tribune*, cor. of Spruce & Nassau, and the *N. Y. Times*, City Hall square, junction of Nassau St. & Park Row, East side of City Hall Park.

LIBRARIES,

OPEN TO VISITORS DURING DAY:

Astor Place, located in Lafayette Place near Astor Place.

Free Academy, located cor. of East 23d St. & Lexington Av. ;

City Hall, located Room 12, City Hall ;

N. Y. Historical Society, 2d Av., cor. of E. 11th St.;

Printers', (over 4,000 volumes), No. 3. Chambers St.

Table of Distances in New York.

From Battery to Trinity Church ¼ mile
,,   ,,   ,, City Hall   ¾ ,,

From Battery			From City Hall	
to Canal St.	1¼	mile	½	mile
,, Houston	1¾	,,	1	,,
,, 9th Street	2¼	,,	1½	,,
,, 19th ,,	2¾	,,	2	,,
,, 29th ,,	3¼	,,	2½	,,
,, 38th ,,	3¾	,,	3	,,
,, 49th ,,	4¼	,,	3½	,,
,, 58th ,,	4¾	,,	4	,,
,, 68th ,,	5¼	,,	4½	,,
,, 78th ,,	5¾	,,	5	,,
,, 88th ,,	6¼	,,	5½	,,
,, 97th ,,	6¾	,,	6	,,
,, 107th ,,	7¼	,,	6½	,,
,, 117th ,,	7¾	,,	7	,,
,, 126th ,,	8¼	,,	Harlem 7½	..

At Harlem you can take a steamboat and in half an hour, after a very pleasant sail, be landed at *High Bridge.* This huge structure supports the Croton aqueduct across the Harlem river ; it is one hundred feet high and one-third of a mile in length, and is supported by fourteen arches. It will well repay a visit.

LIST OF FERRIES.

To Brooklyn, L. I., East river,

foot of Jackson St.,
   ,, ,, Catharine St.,
   ,, ,, Roosevelt St.,
   ,, ,, Fulton St.,
   ,, ,, Wall St.
            South Ferry,
Whitehall (near Battery),

To East Brooklyn, formerly Williamsburg,
foot of Grand St. and foot of East Houston St.

To Green Point, East river,
foot of 10th & E. 23d St.

To South Brooklyn, East river,
Hamilton Av., foot of Whitehall (near Battery),

Staten Island,
foot of Whitehall.

Hoboken, N. J., North river,
foot of Barclay St. (down town),
„ „ Canal „
„ „ Christopher St. (up town).

Jersey City, North river,
foot of Courtlandt St.,
„ „ Desbrosses.

Weehawken, N. R.,
„ „ W. 42d St.

LOCATION OF PIERS.

The North and East River R. R. Line of Cars
(Western Division) pass these Piers.

NORTH RIVER.

No.	STREET.	No.	STREET.
1,	Battery Place	22, 23, 24,	Fulton and Vesey
2, 3,	Battery Place and Morris	25,	Vesey
		26,	Vesey and Barclay
4,	Morris	27,	Robinson
5, 6, 7,	Morris and Rector	28,	Murray
8,	Rector	29,	Warren
9, 10,	Rector and Carlisle	30,	Chambers
11,	Carlisle	31,	Duane
12,	Albany	32,	Duane and Jay
13,	Albany and Cedar	33,	Jay
14,	Cedar	34,	Harrison
15,	Liberty	35,	Franklin
16,	Liberty and Courtlandt	36,	North Moore
17, 18,	Courtlandt	37,	Beach
19,	Courtlandt and Dey	38,	Hubert
20,	Dey	39,	Vestry
21,	Fulton	40,	Watts

No.	STREET.	No.	STREET.
41,	Hoboken	51,	Christopher
42,	Canal	52,	W. Tenth
43,	Spring	53,	Charles
44,	Spring and Charlton	54,	Perry
45,	Charlton	55,	Hammond
46,	King	56,	Bank
47,	West Houston	57,	West Twelfth
48,	Clarkson	58,	Gansevoort
49,	Leroy	59,	Gansevoort and W. 13th
50,	Morton	60,	W. Thirteenth.

EAST RIVER.

No.	STREET.	No.	STREET.
1, 2,	Whitehall.	22,	Fulton.
3,	Moore.	23,	Beckman.
4,	Moore and Broad.	24,	Beckman and Peck Slip.
5,	Broad and Coenties Slip.	25, 26,	Peck Slip.
6, 7, 8,	Coenties Slip.	27,	Dover.
9, 10,	Coenties & Old Slips.	28,	Dover and Roosevelt.
11, 12,	Old Slip.	29,	Roosevelt.
13,	Old Slip & Gouv'r Lane.	30,	Roosevelt & James Slip.
14,	Jones Lane.	31, 32,	James Slip.
15, 16,	Wall.	33,	Oliver.
17,	Pine.	34, 35,	Catharine,
18,	Maiden Lane.	36,	Catharine and Market.
19,	Fletcher.	37, 38,	Market.
20, 21,	Burling Slip.	39,	Market and Pike.

No.	STREET.	No.	STREET.
40, 41,	Pike.	56, 57,	Broome.
42,	Pike and Rutgers.	58, 59,	Delancey.
43, 44,	Rutgers.	60,	Rivington.
45,	Rutgers and Jefferson.	61,	Rivington and Stanton.
46,	Jefferson.	62,	Stanton.
47,	Jefferson and Clinton.	63,	East Houston.
48,	Clinton.	64,	Fifth.
49,	Clinton and Montgomery.	65,	Sixth.
50,	Montgomery.	66,	Seventh.
51, 52,	Gouverneur.	67,	Eighth.
53,	Jackson.	68,	Ninth.
54,	Corlears.	69,	Tenth.
55,	Cherry.	70,	East Eleventh,

POST OFFICES,

open at half past 7 o'clock A. M., closed at 7 P. M.
PRINCIPAL OFFICE,
corner of Nassau St., between Liberty & Cedar Sts.

STATIONS,
remain open until 9 o'clock, P. M.

A. 129 Spring, down town.

B. 439 Grand, East side.

C. cor. of West 12th & 4th St.,
D. Bible House, 8th St., btw. 3d & 4th Av.,
E. 368 8th Av., West side,
F. 408 3d Av.
G. 1259 Broadway, up town.

STEAM R. R. DEPOTS.

CAMDEN & AMBOY, by ferry, foot of Barclay St., North river.

ERIE, foot of Chambers St., Pavonia Ferry, N. R.

HUDSON RIVER, corner of Chambers St. & College Place (down town), and West 30th St., near North river (up town).

NEW JERSEY CENTRAL, by ferry, foot of Courtlandt St., North river.

NORTHERN R. R. OF NEW JERSEY, foot of Courtlandt St., North river.

———— ◆ ————

NEW JERSEY TRANSPORTATION, foot of Courtlandt St., down town, and also Desbrosses Street, (up town) North river.

NEW YORK & HARLEM, cor. of 4th Av. and East 26th St. (up town).

NEW YORK & NEW HAVEN, cor. of 4th Av. and East 27th St. (up town).

LONG ISLAND, James Slip, near foot of Chambers St., E. R.

TO BOSTON via FALL RIVER, steamboat from Pier No. 3. N. R.

TO BOSTON via STONINGTON AND PROVIDENCE, steamboat from the foot of Courtlandt St.

MARKETS.

FULTON MARKET, Fulton, corner South St.

WASHINGTON MARKET, Fulton, corner West St.

CATHARINE MARKET, foot of Catharine St.

CHELSEA MARKET, Ninth Avenue, near Eighteenth Street.

JEFFERSON MARKET, Sixth Avenue, corner Greenwich St.

CLINTON MARKET, Canal, corner West St.

TOMPKINS MARKET, Third Avenue, corner Sixth St.

CENTRE MARKET, Grand, corner Centre St.

PRINCIPAL EXPRESS COMPANIES

ADAMS' EXPRESS, 59 and 442 Broadway.

AMERICAN EXPRESS, 61 Hudson, 124 and 648 Broadway.

BALDWIN, AUSTIN & Co., 72 Broadway.

BOLDT, CHARLES H., 37½ West Thirtieth Street.

BUNTING, CHARLES A., 634 Broadway.

CORWIN & MUNSELL, 72 Broadway and 5 James Slip.

DAVENPORT, MASON & Co., 74 Broadway.

DEFOREST, CHARLES S., foot of Whitehall and Pier 19, N. R.

GROVER, ARTHUR, 117 John and 60 Warren.

HARNDEN'S, 65 and 442 Broadway.

HUSTED, JEROME, 93 Maiden Lane and 66 Courtlandt.

KINGSLEY & Co., 72, 416, and 442 Broadway.

LIBBY, JAMES L., 169 Broadway.

NATIONAL, 65 and 416 Broadway.

NOBBE BROTHERS & Co., 42 and 44 Nassau. European Express.

OGDEN, JOHN T., 66 Courtlandt.

PEOPLE's EXPRESS Co., 63 and 416 Broadway.

PULLEN & Co., *via* N. Y. and H. R. R., 2 Tryon Row.

ROMMEL, JOHN, 67 Courtlandt.

SPAULDING, MORRIS B., 2 Astor House.

STUDLEY, HIRAM, 282 Canal and East Twenty-seventh, corner Fourth Avenue.

UNITED STATES, 82, 291, and 416 Broadway.

WELLS, FARGO & Co., 84 Broadway.

WESTCOTT's 162, 785, and 945 Broadway.

YORKVILLE AND HARLEM EXPRESS.

TELEGRAPH COMPANIES.

AMERICAN TELEGRAPH COMPANY, 145, 293, 580, 673, 721, and 945 Broadway, Astor House, East Seventeenth, corner of Fourth Avenue, Fifth Avenue corner of West Twenty-third, East Forty-fourth near Fourth Avenue, Fourth Avenue corner of East Twenty-seventh, Fourth Avenue corner of East Twenty-sixth, 95 Eighth Avenue, 50 Pine, and 53 Beaver.

ERIE RAILWAY, 189 West.

INDEPENDENT, 26 Nassau, 26 Exchange Place, 18 William, and 513 Broadway.

NEW YORK, ALBANY AND BUFFALO, 145 and 515 Broadway, 28 Pearl, 68 Warren, and West Thirtieth, near Tenth Avenue.

PEOPLE'S, 2 Broad, 21 Wall, 25 William, and Broadway corner of West Twenty-third.

UNITED STATES, 26 Nassau, 26 Exchange Place, 18 William, 31 Pearl, and 513 Broadway.

WESTERN UNION, 145 and 515 Broadway, 68 Warren, 28 Pearl, and West Thirtieth near Tenth Avenue.

www.ingramcontent.com/pod-product-compliance
Lightning Source LLC
Chambersburg PA
CBHW021451090426
42739CB00009B/1721